FALL DOWN SEVEN TIMES, STAND UP EIGHT

Patsy Takemoto Mink and the Fight for Title IX

Written by **Jen Bryant**   Illustrated by **Toshiki Nakamura**

Quill Tree Books
An Imprint of HarperCollins Publishers

Patsy Takemoto was surrounded by water.
On the island of Maui, it was everywhere:
in the creeks that trickled down from the mountains,
in the pools where she splashed with her brother,
in the wide waves of the ocean . . .

. . . and in the ditches that her father designed,
crisscrossing the fields of sugarcane, helping the plants to grow.
Patsy's grandparents came from Japan.
Her grandfather worked in the fields, ran a store, and delivered mail
so the family could have a better life.

Patsy knew that "a better life" also had something to do with school and with the piece of paper that hung over her father's desk.

The Regents of

University of Hawai'i

have conferred upon

Suematsu Takemoto

the Degree of

Bachelor of Science

Civil Engineering

with all its privileges and obligations

Given at Honolulu, Hawai'i

And so, when her older brother, Eugene, started school, young Patsy followed him right in!

At home, Patsy learned about traditions like the Daruma doll:
how to paint in one eye, work hard for a goal,
and then paint in the other eye to show you reached it.
When she touched the doll, it rolled over . . . but then it sprang right back!

Fall down seven times, stand up eight.

It was an old Japanese saying that means never give up!

A few years later, Patsy and Eugene took a train to a school where most of the students were white.

At night, they listened
to President Roosevelt's "fireside chats."

Let us **unite** in banishing fear!

Together we cannot fail.

It was a time known as the Great Depression: Banks closed, parents lost their jobs, and children went hungry. Especially on the mainland, families suffered.

Things were changing in Hawaii, too.

At Maui High School, Patsy joined the debate team.
She surprised everyone with her big ideas and her strong, confident voice.

On December 6, 1941, Patsy celebrated her fourteenth birthday. But the next day . . .

Japan attacked Pearl Harbor, the naval base near Honolulu, Hawaii,
destroying American battleships, buildings, and planes.
More than 3,500 people were killed or injured. It felt like the end of the world.

When President Roosevelt came on the radio, there was hope:
"No matter how long it will take us . . . the American people . . . will win."

Fall down seven times, stand up eight.

The United States declared war on Japan.

Suddenly everything Japanese was suspicious.

Police searched the homes of Japanese Americans, looking for spies or hidden codes.

When they came for Patsy's father, she held on tightly.

Would she ever see him again?

The radio said whole families on the mainland

were being put into prison camps—just for being Japanese.

Patsy's father returned unharmed. But that evening,
he destroyed many family letters and photographs from Japan.

During the war, Patsy and Eugene dug trenches, worked in the cane fields, and made clothing for the soldiers. Patsy organized her classmates.

She was elected the first female student president.
At graduation, she had the best grades in her class.

"I'm going to be a doctor someday," she told her family.

When the war ended, she went to college in Nebraska,
where she missed the wide waves, beaches, and palm trees.
But Patsy was determined to stay on the mainland and finish her education.

"Welcome to the International House!" said the students from Turkey, Hong Kong, and India.

Was there some mistake? Patsy wondered. She was not an international student.

Then she noticed: All the Black, Hispanic, and Asian American students lived there, too.

I live here because I'm not white, she realized. *And that's not right!*

Patsy wrote letters to the newspaper.

She entered a speech contest, arguing against segregation.

She talked to people in coffee shops and in the hallways after class.
People listened to Patsy. The university listened, too. They made a new rule:
White students and students of color would no longer live separately.

Fall down seven times, stand up eight.

At graduation, her dream of becoming a doctor seemed real.
She applied to twenty medical schools.
She waited.

One by one, the envelopes came.

One by one, the medical schools said . . . NO.

"We don't accept women," the schools explained.

Even though her grades were better than most of the men's,
it didn't matter.

Unless the laws changed, women would never be equal, she knew.

What could she do?

Fall down seven times, stand up eight.

The letter from the University of Chicago was crisp and white.
Patsy held her breath: She was accepted to law school!

There was just one other woman in her law school class.
Students were expected to answer any questions the professors asked.

To relax, Patsy played card games. John Mink, a geology student, came to play, too.
Patsy liked him right away. They went out on dates and fell in love.
That winter, in the University chapel, John and Patsy said, "I do."

They graduated in June, and John found a job.

Patsy's male classmates also found jobs.

But despite her good grades, no one hired Patsy.

Fall down seven times, stand up eight.

For a fresh start, the Minks moved back to Hawaii.
Now, with baby Wendy and Patsy's own law office,
there was plenty to do.

One day a friend invited her to a political meeting.
Patsy listened as everyone talked and debated.

She added her own voice to theirs and became a leader.
In 1954, she helped Hawaii Democrats win their elections.

"Politics" was really just a mix of people, words, ideas, and action. Patsy loved it.
"Why don't you run next time?" John asked.
Why not? Patsy thought.

No one else thought she could win, but Patsy walked all across
the island of Oahu—knocking on doors, shaking hands,
and promising to work hard for everyone.

In 1956, Patsy Mink became the first Japanese American woman
elected to the Hawaiian legislature.
She was elected to the territorial Senate in 1958.

Dan K.
INOUYE
US CONGRESS

The following year, Hawaii became the fiftieth state.
It was a big, important step! Now Hawaiians would elect
representatives to the US Congress.
Patsy ran, but the Democrats chose a young war hero instead.

Fall down seven times, stand up eight.

The next summer, Patsy was chosen to speak
at the Democratic National Convention in Los Angeles.

How can America stand as the land of golden opportunity if indeed there is only that opportunity for some and not all.

Her words convinced the Democrats to strengthen their support for civil rights so that every American might have equal access to jobs, education, and voting.

Back in Hawaii, friends and family urged her to try a second time for Congress. Patsy hesitated. *What if I lose again?* she thought.

She bought a special Daruma doll. She painted in one eye. She worked harder than ever. She knocked on doors and shook people's hands. John and Wendy helped, too.

Election day came. The votes were counted . . .

. . . Patsy won!

On January 4, 1965, Patsy Takemoto Mink became
the first woman of color in the US Congress.

Patsy got right to work.
Of the 535 members of Congress, only 13 were female.

Patsy received many letters from women who had been rejected
from colleges or graduate schools because of their gender.
Smart and hardworking, they were turned away.

Along with Representative Edith Green and Senator Birch Bayh,
Patsy cosponsored a bill that required schools to treat men and women equally.
Title IX (nine), as it was called, was just thirty-seven words:

No person in the United States shall, on the basis of sex, be excluded
from participation in, be denied the benefits of, or be subject to
discrimination under any educational program or activity receiving
Federal financial assistance.

Making a law was like drawing a map, Patsy realized.
If a map was drawn well, it led you to a new place.
If a law was written well, it changed lives.

The thirty-seven words of Title IX were part of a large education bill.

In 1971, it passed the Senate, and the following year, it passed the House.
On June 23, 1972, President Richard Nixon signed the bill into law.

But soon there were challenges.
Schools and universities knew that Title IX required them
to give equal opportunity to males and females
as students and as teachers.

And as athletes.

When they heard this, college football and basketball coaches were furious.
A Texas senator agreed with the coaches. He wrote a bill that, if it became a law,
would allow these big-money teams to keep everything for themselves.

Many male lawmakers supported the bill.
They didn't think of women as real athletes. They didn't believe that women
deserved the same opportunities as men.

Patsy sprang into action, calling on every woman in the House of Representatives to make sure that Title IX wasn't weakened by taking out sports.

Patsy presided over the House debate.

Suddenly a man interrupted with an urgent message.

Patsy rushed out of the room . . .

. . . and then to the hospital to be with Wendy, who had been in a car accident.

Without Patsy, the amendment to keep sports as a part of Title IX lost—by one vote.

Fall down seven times, stand up eight.

But this wasn't the end. The Senate still had to vote.
Patsy couldn't be with the congresswomen now . . .

. . . but their hard work paid off. The Senate voted to keep sports as a part of Title IX.

Now, like a tennis ball, the amendment bounced back to the House.
A second vote was taken. And this time . . .

. . . Title IX survived. The congresswomen celebrated.
Patsy's family celebrated, too. Wendy was getting better.

And now that Title IX was passed, all young women
would be treated equally with men—as students and as athletes.

Title IX was a tremendous victory. But there was more to do!
As often as she could, Patsy flew back to Hawaii
to listen to the people who elected her
and to visit with family. Now she understood
that "a better life" also meant "an equal life."

Patsy spent the rest of her life
making sure we ALL have one.

AUTHOR'S NOTE

"There are so many ways in which sex discrimination manifests itself in the form of social custom . . . that you really have to make an issue, whenever it strikes, to protest it. You can't tolerate it."
—Patsy T. Mink

When four-year-old Patsy Takemoto followed her older brother into his classroom on the first day of school, everyone laughed. *She'll get tired of it and quit,* the adults predicted. But Patsy proved she belonged there. Years later, when she ran for the Hawaiian legislature, no one in her male-dominated Democratic Party thought she could win. But Patsy convinced people she could do a better job than the men—and she won.

And when, as a US Congresswoman, she cosponsored a bill that required schools receiving government funds to treat men and women equally, few believed it would pass. But it did. In the years after Title IX was signed into law, millions of women entered colleges and universities previously closed to them. They attended medical schools and law schools in equal numbers with men. They competed in high school and college sports and as professional athletes.

And they could do all of that because of Patsy Mink. "I suppose the purpose of my bill is to free the human spirit to make it possible for everyone to achieve according to their talents and wishes," she explained. As a high school scholar athlete, as a college student, as a wife-mother-teacher-graduate student—I certainly benefitted from Title IX. I imagine most of you have, too. In 2002, Congress renamed Title IX the Patsy T. Mink Equal Opportunity in Education Act. In doing so, they honored the courage and honesty of a young girl who knew, before anyone else did, that she belonged.

—J.B.

ACKNOWLEDGMENTS

The author wishes to thank the following individuals for sharing their time and expertise: Gwendolyn Mink, scholar, author, director of the Patsy T. Mink Education Foundation; Karen Blumenthal, author, Dallas, TX; Loretta Deaver and Patrick Kerwin, Manuscript Reference Librarians, Manuscript Division, Library of Congress, Washington, DC; Mutahara Mobashar, Sr. Information and Reference Specialist, Office of Business Enterprises, Library of Congress, Washington, DC; Alexandra Cooper, Executive Editor, HarperCollins Children's Books; Rachel Zegar, book designer; Laura Harshberger, copy editor; Alyssa E. Henkin, Literary Agent, Birch Path Literary; Toshiki Nakamura, artist.

TIMELINE

December 6, 1927: Patsy Matsu Takemoto is born in Paia (pah-ee-ah), Maui, Hawaii Territory, US, to Suematsu Takemoto and Mitama Tateyama.

1928: Family moves to Hamakuapoko, Maui, where Suematsu works as a sugar plantation engineer.

1931–1932: Patsy has surgery for appendicitis. Follows brother Eugene to school and remains in his class.

1936–1939: Student at Kaunoa English Standard School. Attends political rallies with her father.

1940–1944: Attends Maui HS and participates on debate and public speaking teams. Elected first female student body president. Class valedictorian.

1944–1945: Attends U of Hawaii, Honolulu. President of Pre-Med Students Club and debate team member.

1946–1947: Transfers to Wilson College in Pennsylvania, and later to U of Nebraska, Lincoln. Oversees successful student campaign against campus housing segregation.

September 1947-May 1948: Due to thyroid illness, returns to and graduates from U of Hawaii. Denied admission to medical schools because of her gender.

Summer 1948: Works as a typist. Accepted to U of Chicago Law School under the "foreign student" quota.

Fall 1948–Fall 1950: Attends U of Chicago Law School, one of only two women in a class of ninety.

1951: Marries John Francis Mink in January and finishes law school in May. Applies to Chicago law firms but none will hire a married Asian American woman.

March 6, 1952: Daughter Gwendolyn ("Wendy") Rachel Matsu Mink is born.

August 1952–June 1953: Minks move to Honolulu. Denied application to take the bar exam in Hawaii because she's legally a resident of her husband's home state, Pennsylvania. Patsy challenges the law, wins, and passes the bar.

1953: Opens law office and teaches at U of Hawaii. Attends first political meeting.

1954–1955: Leads the Oahu Young Democrats. Serves as a staff lawyer for the Hawaii legislature.

1956–1958: Elected to the territorial House of Representatives, becoming the first Japanese American woman to serve in the legislature. Elected to the territorial Senate and chairs the Education Committee.

1959–1960: Hawaii becomes a state and Daniel Inouye wins the single congressional seat.

July 1960: Speaker for civil rights at the Democratic National Convention in Los Angeles.

January 3, 1965–January 3, 1971: Member of US House of Representatives from Hawaii's at-large district (elected in 1964).

January 27, 1970: Testifies before the Senate Judiciary Committee to oppose Judge G. Harrold Carswell for the US Supreme Court. Harry Blackmun is confirmed instead, paving the way for his 1973 majority opinion for *Roe v. Wade*.

January 3, 1971–January 3, 1977: Member of the US House of Representatives, Hawaii's 2nd District.

1972: Becomes first Asian American woman to seek the Democratic presidential nomination.

June 23, 1972: Title IX of the Education Amendments Act is signed by President Richard Nixon.

May 20, 1974: Thanks to fierce opposition by Patsy and others, the Tower amendment, which proposes exempting money-making sports from complying with Title IX, fails.

December 1, 1982–December 1, 1986: Honolulu City Council Member, District 9.

September 22, 1990–September 28, 2002: Member of the US House of Rep. from Hawaii's 2nd District.

September 28, 2002: Dies of viral pneumonia in Honolulu, Hawaii, at age 74. Shortly thereafter, Title IX is renamed the Patsy T. Mink Equal Opportunity in Education Act.

2003: The Patsy T. Mink Education Foundation for Low-Income Women and Children is established.

November 24, 2014: President Barack Obama awards Mink a posthumous Medal of Freedom, the nation's highest civilian honor.

SELECTED BIBLIOGRAPHY

Arinaga, Esther K., and Rene E. Ojiri. "Patsy Takemoto Mink." *Asian-Pacific Law & Policy Journal.* Volume 4, no. 2, Summer 2003. pp. 571-597.

Blumenthal, Karen. *Let Me Play: The Story of Title IX, the Law That Changed the Future of Girls in America.* Atheneum Books for Young Readers, 2005.

Engledow, Jill. *Sugarcane Days—Remembering Maui's Hawaiian Commercial & Sugar Company.* Maui Island Press, 2016.

"Gwendolyn Mink Oral History Interview," Office of the Historian, US House of Representatives, March 14, 2016.

"Mink, Patsy Takemoto." United States House of Representatives: History, Art, and Archives. https://history.house.gov/People/detail/18329

Patsy Mink Education Foundation for Low-Income Women and Children. https://www.patsyminkfoundation.org/about-patsy-mink

"Patsy Takemoto Mink." *Former Members of Congress 1955-1976.* https://www.govinfo.gov/content/pkg/GPO-CDOC-108hdoc226/pdf/GPO-CDOC-108hdoc226-2-4-5.pdf

Patsy T. Mink Oral History Interview, 1979. Fern Ingersoll. Box 8, Former Members of Congress, Inc., Oral History Interviews, Manuscript Division, Library of Congress, Washington, DC.

Patsy T. Mink Papers at the Library of Congress. *https://www.loc.gov/rr/mss/mink/mink-about.html*

Ware, Susan. *Title IX: A Brief History with Documents.* Waveland Press, 2014.

NOTES

"[Patsy] was a giant . . . speak out for them." Oct. 1, 2002. Patsy T. Mink memorial transcript, p.7. https://www.govinfo.gov/content/pkg/CPRT-107JPRT82489/html/CPRT-107JPRT82489.htm

"Let us unite in banishing fear." "Together we cannot fail." President Franklin Delano Roosevelt's 1st "Fireside Chat" Radio Address. March 12, 1933. https://www.fdrlibrary.org/documents/356632/390886/First+Fireside+Chat+Speech+Text.pdf/2015e23d-d0dd-49f4-b038-7fdf45cfaf9c, p. 3.

"No matter how long it will take us . . . the American people . . . will win." FDR, Dec. 8, 1941, Congressional Request for Declaration of War. http://docs.fdrlibrary.marist.edu/tmirhdee.html

"I'm going to be a doctor . . ." *Patsy Mink: Ahead of the Majority.* Kimberlee Bassford, writer-director; Making Waves Films, 2008. DVD, 6:35.

"How can America stand as the land of golden opportunity, if indeed there is only that opportunity for some and not all?" Patsy T. Mink, undated handwritten notes for speech given in support of civil rights plank at the Democratic National Convention, Los Angeles, California, July 12, 1960, Container 5, folder 2, Patsy T. Mink Papers, Manuscript Division, Library of Congress. https://www.loc.gov/rr/mss/mink-transcript.html

"There are so many ways in which sex discrimination manifests itself in the form of social custom . . . that you really have to make an issue, whenever it strikes, to protest it. You can't tolerate it." Patsy T. Mink, Oral History Interview, March 6, 1979; March 26, 1979; June 7,1979; USAFMOC, Manuscripts Division, Library of Congress, Washington, DC; p. 111.

"I suppose the purpose of my bill is to free the human spirit to make it possible for everyone to achieve according to their talents and wishes." *Interview with Congresswomen Martha Griffiths and Patsy Mink*—National Archives and Records Administration. https://archive.org/details/gov.archives.arc.39784

For Karen Blumenthal (1959–2020), author and friend

—J.B.

To Mom and Grandmas

—T.N.

Quill Tree Books is an imprint of HarperCollins Publishers.   Fall Down Seven Times, Stand Up Eight: Patsy Takemoto Mink and the Fight for Title IX

Text copyright © 2022 by Jen Bryant   Illustrations copyright © 2022 by Toshiki Nakamura   All rights reserved. Manufactured in Italy.

For information address HarperCollins Children's Books, a division of HarperCollins Publishers, 195 Broadway, New York, NY 10007.   www.harpercollinschildrens.com

ISBN 978-0-06-295722-1

The artist used Photoshop to create the digital illustrations for this book.   Typography by Rachel Zegar   21 22 23 24 25   RTLO   10 9 8 7 6 5 4 3 2 1   ❖ First Edition